CROCHET
LACY SHAWLS

27 ORIGINAL WRAPS *with a* VINTAGE VIBE

ROHN STRONG

STACKPOLE BOOKS
Guilford, Connecticut

Stackpole Books
An imprint of The Rowman & Littlefield Publishing Group, Inc.
4501 Forbes Blvd., Ste. 200, Lanham, MD 20706
Distributed by NATIONAL BOOK NETWORK
800-462-6420

Photography by Harrison Stone

We have made every effort to ensure the accuracy and completeness of these instructions. We cannot, however, be responsible for human error, typographical mistakes, or variations in individual work.

British Library Cataloguing in Publication Information Available

Library of Congress Cataloging-in-Publication Data

Names: Strong, Rohn, author.
Title: Crochet lacy shawls : 27 original wraps with a vintage vibe / Rohn Strong.
Description: Guilford, Connecticut : Rowman & Littlefield Publishing Group, Inc., [2018] | Includes index.
Identifiers: LCCN 2018005256 (print) | LCCN 2018006729 (ebook) | ISBN 9780811767576 (e-book) | ISBN 9780811717861 (pbk. : alk. paper)
Subjects: LCSH: Crocheting—Patterns. | Shawls.
Classification: LCC TT825 (ebook) | LCC TT825 .S785 2018 (print) | DDC 746.43/4—dc23
LC record available at https://lccn.loc.gov/2018005256

CONTENTS

INTRODUCTION

Hey y'all!

I've crocheted my entire life, and I always come back to shawls. I am a shawl guy through and through. After years of practice I've gained a special knowledge and a bit of insight into making and designing crocheted shawls.

A few years ago I decided I wanted to put together a collection of shawls, from beginner to advanced, that would take any crocheter from first stitch to finished shawl. This book is a collection of patterns that show the varying ways crocheted shawls can be completed. It is divided by type of shawl construction, such as top-down triangle, and a beginner, intermediate, and advanced pattern is given for each construction. It is by no means a complete list, but I hope I've grazed the surface.

I recommend you work through this book at your own pace, picking out projects that suit your individual talents, specialties, styles, and tastes. There are patterns for every skill level, and they vary from quick and easy to detailed and intricate. Rest assured, however, each pattern is completely approachable. I've designed 27 patterns that will keep you warm, add a bit of style, and, most importantly, add some skills to your crochet toolbox.

One last note: Because yarns and colorways come and go, some of the yarns and colors used in the samples in this book have been discontinued. I've taken a great deal of effort to suggest similar yarns in similar colors so you may achieve a similar look. I encourage you, however, to really let your creativity soar! Choose your own yarns, your own colors, and design your perfect shawl.

I hope this book will become your go-to resource for crocheted shawls of every shape and style.

Rohn

Beginner

Intermediate

Advanced

BOTTOM-UP TRIANGLE SHAWLS

Triangle shawls are, quite possibly, the most popular shawls out there. Whether knitting, crocheting, or loom knitting, they seem to take center stage. In this section you'll find a variety of bottom-up triangle shawls, beginning with a small number of stitches and increasing out to create the wingspan.

In this chapter you'll find a simple filet crocheted shawl to begin with. Then we use a variegated yarn to bump up a shawl worked in a few different directions. The final shawl in this chapter features a bright yarn and easy-to-memorize stitch pattern for a fun and flirty spring shawl.

BASIC BOTTOM-UP TRIANGLE SHAWL

Triangle shawls are classic and effortlessly easy to wear. Bottom-up triangles offer a different way to shape this versatile shawl.

SKILL LEVEL
Beginner

FINISHED MEASUREMENTS
Wingspan: 48 in. (122 cm)
Depth: 24 in. (61 cm)

YARN
Lion Brand Yarn LB Collection Angora Merino (80% extrafine merino wool, 20% angora; 131 yd./120 m per 1.75 oz./50 g skein)
- 2 skeins Avocado

HOOK & OTHER MATERIALS
- US J-10 (6 mm) crochet hook
- Yarn needle
- Scissors

GAUGE
In pattern stitch (filet double crochet: dc, ch 1, dc), 5 sts x 3 rows = 2 in. (5 cm) square
Adjust hook size if necessary to obtain gauge.

NOTES
- Beg Ch 4 counts as (dc, ch 1) throughout.

Instructions

Ch 4.

Row 1: 3 dc in 4th ch from hook. (3 dc)

Row 2: Ch 4, turn, (dc, ch 1) in each st across to last st; (dc, ch 1, dc) in last st. (5 dc and 4 ch-sps)

Row 3: Ch 4, turn, (dc, ch 1) in each st across to last st; (dc, ch 1, dc) in last st.

Repeat row 3, increasing on each side of every row, until shawl is 48 in. (122 cm) wide, or desired wingspan.

Pin and block to measurements. Weave in ends.

FROST SHAWL

This shawl is all about the interesting construction. It begins bottom-up and then turns into a top-down. It is fun and exciting.

SKILL LEVEL
Intermediate

FINISHED MEASUREMENTS
Wingspan: 48 in. (122 cm)
Depth: 20 in. (51 cm)

YARN
Lion Brand Yarn LB Collection Crepe Melange, worsted-weight yarn
  (50% acrylic, 50% nylon; 173 yd./158 m per 2.6 oz./75 g skein)
  ▪ 5 skeins Cosmos
Alternative Yarn: Any #3 lightweight worsted yarn will work for
  this project.

HOOK & OTHER MATERIALS
  ▪ US J-10 (6 mm) crochet hook
  ▪ Yarn needle
  ▪ Scissors

GAUGE
In half double crochet, 6 sts x 6 rows = 2 in. (5 cm) square
Adjust hook size if necessary to obtain gauge.

NOTES
  ▪ Ch 2 counts as hdc throughout.
  ▪ Ch 4 counts as (dc, ch 1) throughout.

Instructions

Ch 4.

Row 1: 3 dc in 4th ch from hook. (3 dc)

Row 2: Ch 4, turn, sk first st, dc in next st, ch 1, dc in last st. (3 dc and 2 ch)

Row 3: Ch 4, turn, dc in first st, *ch 1, dc in next st; rep from * across to last st, (ch 1, dc) twice in last st. (5 dc and 4 ch)

Rep row 3 until shawl measures 24 in. (61 cm) wide.

Next row: Ch 3, turn piece 90 degrees, place 2 dc inside each dc along both sides of triangle. Place a marker in center stitch near point of triangle.

Next row: Ch 2, turn, 2 hdc in first st, hdc in each st across to 1 st before marker, 2 hdc in next st, hdc in marked st (move up marker), 2 hdc in next st, hdc in each st across to last st, 2 hdc in last st.

Rep last row until shawl measures 48 in. (122 cm) or desired wingspan.

Pin and block to measurements. Weave in ends.

IVY SHAWL

The Ivy Shawl is a sweet and lacy shawl that will bring a touch of fashion to your wardrobe. This piece is all about the drama.

SKILL LEVEL
Advanced

FINISHED MEASUREMENTS
Wingspan: 64 in. (163 cm)
Depth: 18 in. (46 cm)

YARN
Lion Brand Yarn LB Collection Crepe Twist, #4 medium-weight yarn
  (68% wool, 32% nylon; 83 yd./76 m per 1.75 oz./50 g skein)
- 5 skeins Lemongrass

HOOK & OTHER MATERIALS
- US J-10 (6 mm) crochet hook
- Yarn needle
- Scissors

GAUGE
In pattern stitch, 1 rep x 1 row = 1 in. (2.5 cm) square
Adjust hook size if necessary to obtain gauge.

NOTES
- Ch 5 counts as tr throughout.

Instructions

Ch 4.

Row 1: Dc in 4th ch from hook, ch 2, 2 dc in same ch. (4dc, ch-2 sp)

Row 2: Ch 5, turn, (tr, ch 2, 2 tr) in first st, dc in next ch-2 sp, (2 tr, ch 2, 2 tr) in last st. (8 tr, 1 dc, 2 ch-2 sps)

Row 3: Ch 5, turn, (tr, ch 2, 2 tr) in first st, *dc in next ch-2 sp, (2 tr, ch 2, 2 tr) in next dc; rep from * across to last st, (2 tr, ch 2, 2 tr) in last st.

Rep row 3 until shawl measures 64 in. (163 cm) or desired wing-span.

Pin and block to measurements. Weave in ends.

Beginner

Intermediate

Advanced

PI SHAWLS

Traditional pi shawls are worked from the center out. I prefer the half pi shawl, which is what you'll find in this section. Points of increase are separated by rows of pattern, making it a fun and inventive way of customizing your shawl. If the stitch fits, it works!

In this chapter we begin with a filet crochet pattern to get us comfortable with the shape. From there we'll move on to a striking red and green shawl, working in a number of stitches with a gorgeous lace finish. The advanced shawl incorporates three lace stitches in soft, beautiful cashmere yarn, fit for a queen.

BASIC PI SHAWL

Pi shawls are the simplest of all crochet shawl shapes. Worked in allover filet crochet, this shawl makes a quick and easy lace accent piece.

SKILL LEVEL
Beginner

FINISHED MEASUREMENTS
Wingspan: 48 in. (122 cm)
Depth: 16.5 in. (42 cm)

YARN
Lion Brand Yarn Tweed Stripes, worsted-weight yarn (100% acrylic; 144 yd./132 m per 3 oz./85 g skein)
- 1 skein Popsicle

HOOK & OTHER MATERIALS
- US L-11 (8 mm) crochet hook
- Yarn needle
- Scissors

GAUGE
In double crochet, 6 sts x 2 rows = 2 in. (5 cm) square
Adjust hook size if necessary to obtain gauge.

NOTES
- Ch 4 counts as (dc, ch 1) throughout.

Instructions

Ch 5.

Row 1: Dc into 5th ch from hook, (ch 1, dc) 3 more times. (5 dc and 4 ch-1 sps)

Row 2: Ch 4, turn, dc in first st, *ch 1, (dc, ch 1, dc) in next ch-1 sp; rep from * across, working last rep in top of t-ch. (10dc, 9 ch-1 sps)

Row 3: Ch 4, (ch 1, dc in top of next dc) across.

Row 4: Ch 4, turn, dc in first st, *ch 1, (dc, ch 1, dc) in next dc; rep from * across, working last rep in top of t-ch.

Rows 5–7: Rep row 3.

Row 8: Rep row 4.

Rows 9–15: Rep row 3.

Row 16: Rep row 4.

Rows 17–24: Rep row 3.

Row 25: Sc in each dc and ch sp across. Fasten off.

Note: To make this shawl larger, rep row 3 a further 28 times; then work another increase row. Continue working row 3 for up to 24 more rows. Work row 25 when the shawl is the desired size. Fasten off.

Pin and block to measurements. Weave in ends.

I just love pi shawls. This particular shawl is worked in a few different stitches in a lightweight yarn. A contrasting color is used for a fun and engaging edging.

SKILL LEVEL
Intermediate

FINISHED MEASUREMENTS
Wingspan: 46 in. (117 cm)
Depth: 17 in. (43 cm)

YARN
Lion Brand Yarn LB Collection Crepe Twist, worsted-weight yarn (88% wool, 12% nylon; 112 yd./102 m per 1.75 oz./50 g skein)
- 3 skeins A (Geranium)
- 2 skeins B (Lemongrass)

HOOK & OTHER MATERIALS
- US J-10 (6 mm) crochet hook
- Yarn needle
- Scissors

GAUGE
In half double crochet, 7 sts = 2 in. (5 cm) square
Adjust hook size if necessary to obtain gauge.

NOTES
- Ch 3 counts as dc throughout.
- Ch 4 counts as tr throughout.

Instructions

With A, ch 11.

Row 1 (WS): Sc in 2nd ch from hook and in each ch across. (10 sts)

Row 2 (RS): Ch 1, turn, 2 sc in each st across. (20 sts)

Rows 3–5: Ch 1, turn, sc in each st across.

Row 6: Ch 1, turn, 2 sc in each st across. (40 sts)

Rows 7–10: Ch 2, turn, hdc in each st across.

Row 11: Rep row 6. (80 sts)

Rows 12–17: Ch 3, turn, dc in each st across.

Row 18: Rep row 6. (160 sts)

Rows 19–22: Ch 4, turn, tr in each st across.

Row 23: Ch 2, turn, hdc in each st across.

Row 24 (RS): Join B, ch 4, turn, tr in each st across.

Row 25: Ch 4, turn, (dc, ch 1) in each st across, dc in last dc.

Row 26: Ch 1, turn, sc in each of the first 2 ch-1 sps, *ch 2, sk next ch-1 sp, (2 dc, ch 2, 2 dc) in next ch-2 sp, ch 2, sk next ch-1 sp, sc in next ch-1 sp; rep from * across, sc in last ch-1 sp.

Row 27: Ch 5, turn, *dc in each of the next 2 dc, 2 dc in ch-2 sp, dc in each of the next 2 dc, ch 2; rep from * across, tr in last st.

Row 28: Ch 3, turn, *dc2tog, ch 2, 2 dc in next dc, ch 2, 2 dc in next dc, ch 2, dc2tog; rep from * across, tr in last st. Fasten off.

Pin and block to measurements. Weave in ends.

HYACINTH SHAWL

This pi shawl combines some of my favorite lace stitches—three to be exact. Each stitch builds on the previous one with ease, and all are a lot of fun to complete!

SKILL LEVEL
Advanced

FINISHED MEASUREMENTS
Wingspan: 44 in. (112 cm)
Depth: 15 in. (38 cm)

YARN
Lion Brand Yarn LB Collection Cashmere, worsted-weight yarn
(100% cashmere; 82 yd./75 m per 0.88 oz./25 g skein)
- 5 skeins Cream

HOOK & OTHER MATERIALS
- US K-10$^{1}/_{2}$ (6.5 mm) crochet hook
- Yarn needle
- Scissors

GAUGE
In pattern stitch (dc, ch 1), 6 sts x 2.5 rows = 2 in. (5 cm) square
Adjust hook size if necessary to obtain gauge.

NOTES
- Ch 3 counts as dc throughout.
- Ch 4 counts as tr throughout.

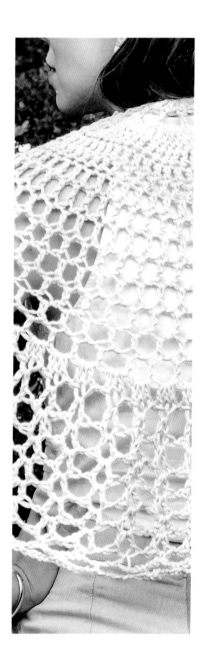

Instructions

Ch 4.

Row 1: 12 dc in 4th ch from hook.

Row 2: Ch 5, turn, *dc in next dc, ch 2, sk next dc; rep from * across, dc in last dc. (7 dc, 6 ch-2 sps).

Row 3: Ch 3, turn, *5 dc in next ch-2 sp, rep from * across, end last rep, 5 dc in next ch-2 sp, dc in last dc. (32 sts)

Rows 4–6: Ch 3, turn, dc in each st across.

Rows 7–13: Ch 4, *dc in next st, ch 1; rep from * across, dc in last dc.

Row 14: Ch 5, *dc in next st, ch 2; rep from * across, dc in last dc.

Row 15: Ch 3, turn, *3 dc in ch-2 sp, ch 1; rep from * across to last ch-2 sp, 3 dc in last ch-2 sp, dc in last dc.

Rows 16–21: Ch 3, turn, dc in each of the first 3 dc, *ch 1, (dc, ch 1, dc) in center st of next 3-dc group; rep from * across to last 4 sts, dc in each st.

Rows 22–23: Ch 5, sk 2 sts, sc in next dc, *ch 5, sc in center ch-1 st of (dc, ch 1, dc) group; rep from * across to last st, dc in last dc. Fasten off.

Pin and block to measurements. Weave in ends.

Beginner

Intermediate

Advanced

STOLES

A stole, the brother of the scarf, is a wide piece of fabric often worked from one end to the other. These are great for covering up when the chill first hits you, or to wrap around into a super scarf. Either way, the stole is my favorite piece to make.

Our first piece is a simple stole worked in a combination of basic crochet stitches to keep it interesting. Following that we have a gorgeous faux fur wrap that will look great on any night out. Lastly, we use Tunisian crochet to close the show, with a simple but lacy edge.

BASIC STOLE

A stole is like a giant oversized scarf. The great thing is that it can be worn like a scarf, a wrap, a shawl, or whatever you'd like!

SKILL LEVEL
Beginner

FINISHED MEASUREMENTS
Wingspan: 72 in. (183 cm)
Depth: 11½ in. (29 cm)

YARN
Lion Brand Yarn Lion's Pride Woolspun (80% acrylic, 20% wool; 124 yd./116 m per 3.5 oz./100 g skein)
- 2 skeins Oxford Grey

HOOK & OTHER MATERIALS
- US J-10 (6 mm) crochet hook
- Yarn needle
- Scissors

GAUGE
In double crochet, 5 sts x 3 rows = 2 in. (5 cm) square
Adjust hook size if necessary to obtain gauge.

NOTES
- Ch 3 counts as dc throughout.
- Ch 4 counts as tr throughout.

Instructions

Ch 33.

Row 1 (RS): Dc in 4th ch from hook and in each ch across. (31 dc)

Row 2 (WS): Ch 4, turn, tr in each st across.

Row 3 (RS): Ch 3, turn, dc in each st across.

Rep rows 2 and 3 until shawl measures 36 in. (91 cm) long. Fasten off.

Return to the foundation row and join yarn to work in the opposite side as follows:

Row 1: Ch 3, dc in each st across.

Row 2: Ch 4, turn, tr in each st across.

Row 3: Ch 3, turn, dc in each st across.

Rep rows 2 and 3 until shawl measures 72 in. (183 cm) long (36 in. [91 cm] each side). Fasten off.

Pin and block to measurements. Weave in ends.

CATTAIL STOLE

This stole, inspired by the cattails I collected as a child, is a great and fun accent piece. Wear it as an oversized scarf or a statement piece with that little black dress.

SKILL LEVEL
Intermediate

FINISHED MEASUREMENTS
Wingspan: 72 in. (183 cm)
Depth: 11 in. (28 cm)

YARN
Lion Brand Yarn Wool-Ease Thick & Quick (80% acrylic, 20% wool; 106 yd./97 m per 6 oz./170 g skein)
- 5 skeins Black

Lion Brand Yarn Pelt Yarn, bulky-weight yarn (68% nylon, 32% polyester; 47 yd./43 m per 1.75 oz./50 g skein)
- 10 skeins Sable

HOOK & OTHER MATERIALS
- US N/P-15 (10 mm) crochet hook
- Yarn needle
- Scissors

GAUGE
In double crochet, 5 sts x 3 rows = 2 in. (5 cm) square
Adjust hook size if necessary to obtain gauge.

NOTES
- Ch 3 counts as dc throughout.
- Ch 4 counts as tr throughout.

Instructions

With 1 strand of each yarn, ch 25.

Row 1: Hdc in 3rd ch from hook and in each ch across. (22 hdc)

Row 2: Ch 3, turn, dc in each st across.

Row 3: Ch 4, turn, tr in each st across.

Row 4: Ch 2, turn, hdc in each st across.

Rep rows 2–4 until piece is desired length.

Pin and block to measurements. Weave in ends.

JORDAN LAKE STOLE

I'm a giant fan of Tunisian crochet. This shawl is completed in separate strips and then seamed. An edging is then worked after all strips are joined.

SKILL LEVEL
Advanced

FINISHED MEASUREMENTS
Wingspan: 65 in. (165 cm)
Depth: 17 in. (43 cm)

YARN
Lion Brand Yarn Wool-Ease, worsted-weight yarn (50% acrylic, 50% cotton; 106 yd./97 m per 6 oz./170 g skein)
- 3 skeins A (Fisherman)
- 1 skein B (Eggplant)

HOOK & OTHER MATERIALS
- US L-11 (8 mm) Tunisian crochet hook
- US J-10 (6 mm) crochet hook
- Yarn needle
- Scissors

GAUGE
In Tunisian double crochet, 5 sts x 2 rows = 2 in. (5 cm) square
Adjust hook size if necessary to obtain gauge.

NOTES
- Ch 3 counts as Tdc throughout.

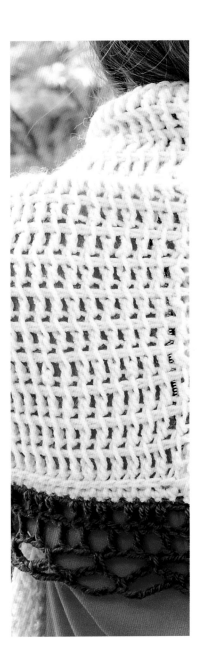

Instructions

TUNISIAN CROCHET SECTION (MAKE 10)

With A and Tunisian crochet hook, ch 20.

Work Tunisian Foundation Row as follows:

Forward Pass: Skip first ch, insert hook under back strand of next ch, yarn over and pull up a loop. Repeat across until 20 loops are on hook.

Return Pass: Yarn over, pull through one loop on hook, yarn over and pull through two loops on hook until you have one loop left on hook and all sts are closed.

Row 1: Tss in each st across. Return pass.

Row 2: Ch 3, Tdc in each st across. Return pass.

Rep row 2 a further 13 times. Fasten off.

Last row: Sc in each st across.

Make all 10 sections and seam at each vertical edge to make a long stole.

Next row: Sc in each st around stole.

TUNISIAN REFRESHER

Tss (Tunisian simple stitch): Insert hook from right to left through next front vertical bar, yarn over and draw up a loop, leaving it on your hook. Continue across the row. On the return pass, yarn over and draw through two loops on the first stitch, and yarn over and draw through one loop on all other stitches until you have one loop left on the hook.

Tdc (Tunisian double crochet): Yarn over, insert the hook from right to left behind the next front vertical bar, yarn over and draw up a loop. Yarn over, and draw through 2 loops on the hook. Leave the final loop of the stitch on the hook. Work the return pass the same as for the Tss.

EDGING

Row 1: With B, join in one corner of long edge of shawl, ch 1, sc in each sc across. (200 sc)

Rows 2–3: Ch 4, turn, *sk next st, dc in next dc, ch 1; rep from * across to last st, dc in last st.

Rows 4–5: Ch 1, turn, sc in first st, *ch 5, sk next ch-1 sp, sc in next ch-1 sp; rep from * across to last ch-1 sp, ch 3, dc in last st. Fasten off.

Pin and block to measurements. Weave in ends.

Beginner

Intermediate

Advanced

COLLARS

The collar is the quintessential accessory if you're look-ing to add a touch of crochet but aren't interested in a large amount of crocheted fabric. Whether basic or lacy, these collars will add a touch of class to your wardrobe.

We'll start with a basic rectangle and shape it how we want; then we'll move on to a simple and chic collar. A lacy number closes this chapter with a burst of color and touch of pineapple.

BASIC COLLAR

A collar is like a mini shawl; it can adorn a sweater or be tucked into a jacket. This collar is a great gift and an even better beginner project.

SKILL LEVEL
Beginner

FINISHED MEASUREMENTS
Wingspan: 23 in. (58 cm)
Depth: 7 in. (18 cm)

YARN
Lion Brand Yarn Vanna's Choice; #4 medium-weight yarn (100% acrylic; 170 yd./156 m per 3.5 oz./100 g skein)
- 1 skein Eggplant

HOOK & OTHER MATERIALS
- US I-9 (5.5 mm) crochet hook
- Yarn needle
- Scissors

GAUGE
In double crochet, 7 sts x 4 rows = 2 in. (5 cm) square
Adjust hook size if necessary to obtain gauge.

NOTES
- Ch 3 counts as dc throughout.

Instructions

Ch 26.

Row 1 (RS): Sc in 2nd ch from hook and in each ch across. (25 sc)

Row 2 (WS): Ch 3, turn, dc in each st across.

Row 3 (RS): Ch 1, turn, sc in each st across.

Rep rows 2 and 3 until collar measures 23 in. (58 cm) long. On last
row, join last st of last row to first st of foundation row.

Pin and block to measurements. Weave in ends.

To wear, simply pull over head like a cowl and fold down collar.

ORANGE MARMALADE COLLAR

This collar is about as sweet and dainty as you can get. It features just a touch of crochet lace in a DK-weight yarn.

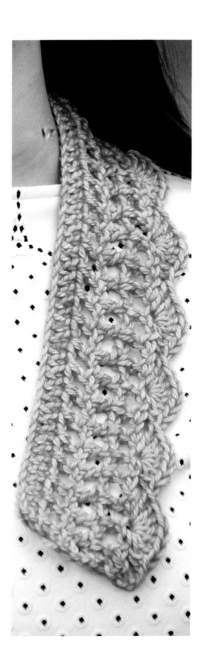

SKILL LEVEL
Intermediate

FINISHED MEASUREMENTS
Wingspan: 24 in. (61 cm)
Depth: 2.5 in. (6 cm)

YARN
Lion Brand Yarn Modern Baby, DK-weight yarn (50% acrylic, 50% nylon; 173 yd./158 m per 2.6 oz./75 g skein)
- 1 skein Apricot

Alternative Yarn: Any #3 DK-weight yarn will work for this project.

HOOK & OTHER MATERIALS
- US I-9 (5.5 mm) crochet hook
- Yarn needle
- Scissors

GAUGE
In double crochet, 8 sts x 4 rows = 2 in. (5 cm) square
Adjust hook size if necessary to obtain gauge.

NOTES
- Ch 3 counts as dc throughout.
- Ch 4 counts as (dc, ch 1) throughout.

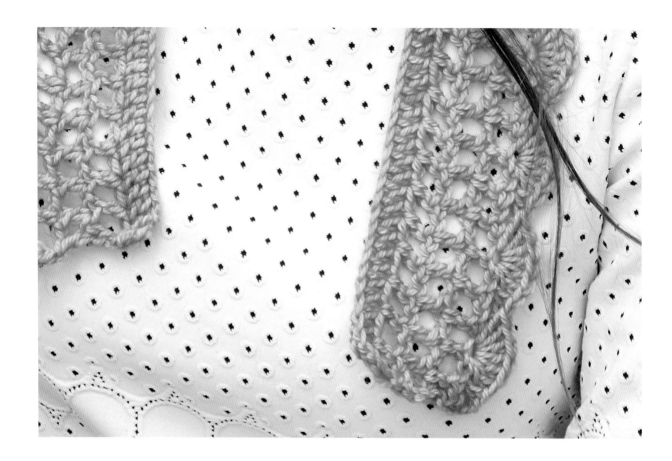

Instructions

Ch 99.

Row 1: Dc in 4th ch from hook and in each ch across. (96 dc)

Row 2: Ch 4, sk next dc, *dc in next dc, ch 1, sk next dc; rep from * across to last st, dc in last dc.

Rep row 2 twice more.

Row 5: Ch 3, sk next 3 sts, *7 dc in next dc, sk next 5 sts; rep from * across to last 5 sts, 7 dc in next dc, sk next 3 sts, dc in last dc). Fasten off.

Pin and block to measurements. Weave in ends.

ORCHID COLLAR

A classic pineapple motif combined with a modern and colorful yarn makes this collar a stunner.

SKILL LEVEL
Advanced

FINISHED MEASUREMENTS
Wingspan: 26 in. (66 cm)
Depth: 7 in. (18 cm)

YARN
Lion Brand Yarn LB Collection Crepe Melange, worsted-weight yarn (50% acrylic, 50% nylon; 173 yd./158 m per 2.6 oz./75 g skein)
- 2 skeins Iris

Alternative Yarn: Any #4 heavy worsted-weight yarn will work for this project.

HOOK & OTHER MATERIALS
- US G-6 (4 mm) crochet hook
- Yarn needle
- Scissors
- 1-in. button

GAUGE
In double crochet, 5 sts x 4 rows = 2 in. (5 cm) square
Adjust hook size if necessary to obtain gauge.

NOTES
- Ch 3 counts as dc throughout.
- Ch 4 counts as (dc, ch 1) throughout.

Ch 105.

Row 1 (RS): Sc in 2nd ch from hook and in each ch across. (104 sc)

Rows 2–9: Ch 1, turn, sc in each sc across. (104 sc)

On last row, ch 1, do not turn to WS.

Turn work 90 degrees to work in ends of rows.

Row 1 (RS): Sc in end of each row across. (9 sc)

Rows 2–9: Ch 1, turn, sc in each sc across. (9 sc)

On last row, ch 1, do not turn to WS.

Turn work 90 degrees to work in opposite end of foundation ch.

Row 1 (RS): Sc in each ch across at the opposite end of foundation ch.

Rows 2–9: Ch 1, turn, sc in each sc across. (104 sc)

On last row, ch 1, do not turn to WS. (104 sc)

Turn work 90 degrees to work in ends of rows.

Row 1 (RS): Sc in end of each row across. (9 sc)

Rows 2–9: Ch 1, turn, sc in each sc across. (9 sc)

On last row, ch 1, do not turn to WS.

Each row is worked from right to left with RS facing. Break yarn at end of each row and rejoin with RS facing.

Row 1: Ch 3, (dc, ch 2, 2 dc) in same stitch as join, *ch 5, sk next 3 sts, sc in next sc, ch 2, sk next 2 sts, sc in next sc, ch 5, sk next 3 sts, (2 dc, ch 2, 2 dc) in next sc; rep from * across.

Row 2: Sl st to first ch-2 sp, ch 3, (dc, ch 2, 2 dc) in next ch-2 sp, *sc in next ch-5 sp, ch 7, sc in next ch-5 sp, ch 2, (2 dc, ch 2, 2 dc) in next ch-2 sp; rep from * across.

Row 3: Sl st to first ch-2 sp, ch 3, (dc, ch 2, 2 dc) in next ch-2 sp, *(dc in next dc, ch 1, sk next dc) 6 times, (2 dc, ch 2, 2 dc) in next ch-2 sp; rep from * across.

Row 4: Sl st to first ch-2 sp, ch 3, (dc, ch 2, 2 dc) in next ch-2 sp, *ch 1, (dc in next ch-1 sp, ch 1) 5 times, ch 1, (2 dc, ch 2, 2 dc) in next ch-2 sp; rep from * across.

Row 5: Sl st to first ch-2 sp, ch 3, (dc, ch 2, 2 dc) in next ch-2 sp, *ch 2, (dc in next ch-1 sp, ch 1) 4 times, ch 2, (2 dc, ch 2, 2 dc) in next ch-2 sp; rep from * across.

Row 6: Sl st to first ch-2 sp, ch 3, (dc, ch 2, 2 dc) in next ch-2 sp, *ch 3, (dc in next ch-1 sp, ch 1) 3 times, ch 3, (2 dc, ch 2, 2 dc) in next ch-2 sp; rep from * across.

Row 7: Sl st to first ch-2 sp, ch 3, (dc, ch 2, 2 dc) in next ch-2 sp, *ch 4, (dc in next ch-1 sp, ch 1) 2 times, ch 4, (2 dc, ch 2, 2 dc) in next ch-2 sp; rep from * across.

Row 8: As row 2.

Row 9: As row 3. Fasten off.

Pin and block to measurements. Weave in ends.

Beginner

Intermediate

Advanced

PONCHOS

The poncho doesn't have to get stuck in the '70s anymore. From the basic poncho to the lacier, cowl-like poncho, these pieces have become an indispensable part of our crochet closet. Try different weights of yarn and different lengths to create more dramatic and unique pieces.

Our first poncho is a super bulky piece to get us started. Super bulky yarn in bright pops of color gives our next shawl a whimsical look and feel. We end with a lacy number that can be worn as a cowl or a poncho … you choose!

BASIC PONCHO

A poncho doesn't have to look like it came straight out of the '70s. This simple but quick-to-stitch poncho is perfect for throwing over a top in the fall.

SKILL LEVEL
Beginner

FINISHED MEASUREMENTS
Circumference: 48 in. (122 cm)
Depth: 10 in. (25 cm)

YARN
Lion Brand Yarn Wool-Ease Thick & Quick, super bulky-weight yarn
(80% acrylic, 20% wool; 106 yd./97 m per 6 oz./170 g skein)
- 1 skein A (Fisherman)
- 1 skein B (Peacock)
- 1 skein C (Navy)

HOOK & OTHER MATERIALS
- US M/N-13 (9 mm) crochet hook
- Yarn needle
- Scissors

GAUGE
In half double crochet, 3 sts x 2 rows = 2 in. (5 cm) square
Adjust hook size if necessary to obtain gauge.

NOTES
- Ch 2 does not count as hdc throughout.
- Change colors as desired.

Instructions

With A, ch 32, join with a sl st to work in the round.

Rnds 1–4: Ch 1, sc in each st around, join with a sl st to first st. (32 sts)

Rnd 5: Ch 2, *hdc in first st, 2 hdc in next st; rep from * around, ending last rep with hdc in last st, join with a sl st to first st. (47 sts)

Rnds 6–7: Ch 2, hdc in each st around, join with a sl st to first st.

Rnd 8: Ch 2, *hdc in first 2 sts, 2 hdc in next st; rep from * around, join with a sl st to first st.

Rep rnds 6–8 twice more.

Pin and block to measurements. Weave in ends.

SHIFTING WAVES PONCHO

This poncho delivers a hit of color with a neutral edge. By taking advantage of stitch height, we are able to achieve the look of waves without much work at all!

SKILL LEVEL
Intermediate

FINISHED MEASUREMENTS
Circumference: 64 in. (163 cm)
Depth: 15 in. (38 cm)

YARN
Lion Brand Yarn Wool-Ease Thick & Quick, super bulky-weight yarn
   (80% acrylic, 20% wool; 106 yd./97 m per 6 oz./170 g skein)
- 3 skeins A (Mustard)
- 2 skeins B (Fisherman)
- 2 skeins C (Eggplant)
- 2 skeins D (Raspberry)

HOOK & OTHER MATERIALS
- US M/N-13 (9 mm) crochet hook
- Yarn needle
- Scissors

GAUGE
In double crochet, 3 sts x 2 rows = 2 in. (5 cm) square
Adjust hook size if necessary to obtain gauge.

NOTE
Beginning chains do not count as stitches throughout.

Instructions

With A, ch 34, join with a sl st to work in the round.

Rnds 1–2: Ch 1, sc in each st around, join with a sl st to first st. (34 sts)

Rnd 3: Ch 1, *2 sc in next sc, sc in next sc; rep from * around, join with a sl st to first st. (51 sts)

Rnd 4: Join B, ch 1, sc in each st around.

Rnd 5: Ch 1, sc in each of the first 20 sts, hdc in each of the next 2 sts, dc in each of the next 2 sts, tr in each of the next 21 sts, dc in each of the next 2 sts, hdc in each of the next 2 sts, sc in each of the last 2 sts.

Rnd 6: Join A, ch 1, *2 sc in next sc, sc in each of the next 2 sc; rep from * around, join with a sl st to first st. (68 sts)

Rnd 7: Join B, ch 1, sc in each of the first 20 sts, hdc in each of the next 2 sts, dc in each of the next 2 sts, tr in each of the next 38 sts, dc in each of the next 2 sts, hdc in each of the next 2 sts, sc in each of the last 2 sts, join with a sl st to first st.

Rnd 8: Join A, ch 1, *2 sc in next sc, sc in each of the next 3 sc; rep from * around, join with a sl st to first st. (85 sts)

Rnd 9: Join C, ch 1, sc in each of the first 20 sts, hdc in each of the next 2 sts, dc in each of the next 2 sts, tr in each of the next 55 sts, dc in each of the next 2 sts, hdc in each of the next 2 sts, sc in each of the last 2 sts, join with a sl st to first st.

Rnd 10: Join A, ch 1, *2 sc in next sc, sc in each of the next 4 sc; rep from * around, join with a sl st to first st, join with a sl st to first st. (102 sts)

Rnd 11: Join C, ch 1, sc in each of the first 20 sts, hdc in each of the next 2 sts, dc in each of the next 2 sts, tr in each of the next 72 sts, dc in each of the next 2 sts, hdc in each of the next 2 sts, sc in each of the last 2 sts, join with a sl st to first st.

Rnd 12: Join A, ch 1, *2 sc in next sc, sc in each of the next 5 sc; rep from * around, join with a sl st to first st, join with a sl st to first st. (119 sts)

Rnd 13: Join D, ch 4, tr in each of the first 20 sts, hdc in each of the next 2 sts, dc in each of the next 2 sts, sc in each of the next 89 sts, dc in each of the next 2 sts, hdc in each of the next 2 sts, sc in each of the last 2 sts, join with a sl st to first st.

Rnd 14: Join A, ch 1, *2 sc in next sc, sc in each of the next 6 sc; rep from * around, join with a sl st to first st, join with a sl st to first st. (136 sts)

Rnd 15: Join D, ch 4, tr in each of the first 20 sts, hdc in each of the next 2 sts, dc in each of the next 2 sts, sc in each of the next 106 sts, dc in each of the next 2 sts, hdc in each of the next 2 sts, sc in each of the last 2 sts, join with a sl st to first st.

Rnds 16–18: Join A, ch 4, tr in each st around, join with a sl st to first st.

Rnd 19: Join D, ch 1, sc in each st around, join with a sl st to first st. Fasten off.

Pin and block to measurements. Weave in ends.

AMARYLLIS PONCHO

Sometimes a poncho can be lacy and light. In this case, amaryllis flowers served as the inspiration for this fun and delicate lace pattern.

SKILL LEVEL
Advanced

FINISHED MEASUREMENTS
Circumference: 64 in. (163 cm)
Depth: 15 in. (38 cm)

YARN
Lion Brand Yarn Vanna's Choice (100% acrylic; 170 yd./156 m per 3.5 oz./100 g skein)
- 2 skeins Fern

HOOK & OTHER MATERIALS
- US H-8 (5 mm) crochet hook
- Yarn needle
- Scissors

GAUGE
In pattern stitch (filet double crochet: dc, ch 1, dc), 3 sts x 2 rows = 2 in. (5 cm) square
Adjust hook size if necessary to obtain gauge.

Instructions

Ch 62, join to work in the round taking care not to twist sts.

Rnd 1: Ch 4, do not turn, *sk next ch, dc in next ch, ch 1; rep from * around, join with a sl st to beg ch.

Rnd 2: Ch 1, sc in fist st, *sk next dc, 7 dc in next dc, sk next dc, sc in next dc; rep from * around to last 2 dc, 7 dc in next dc, sk last dc, join with a sl st to beg ch.

Rnd 3: Ch 4, dc in same st as join, *ch 3, sk next 3 dc, sc in next dc, ch 3, sk next 3 dc, (dc, ch 1, dc) in next sc, ch 3, sk next 3 dc, sc in next dc, ch 3, sk next 3 dc, dc in next sc; rep from * around, end last rep, sc in next dc, ch 3, join with a sl st to beg ch.

Rnds 4–5: Ch 4, *dc in next dc, ch 1, dc in next ch-3 sp, ch 1, dc in next sc, ch 1, dc in next ch-3 sp; rep from * around, join with a sl st to beg ch. (78 sts)

Rnd 6: As rnd 2.

Rnd 7: Ch 4, dc in same st as join, *ch 3, sk next 3 dc, sc in next dc, ch 3, sk next 3 dc, (dc, ch 1, dc) in next sc, (ch 3, sk next 3 dc, sc in next dc, ch 3, sk next 3 dc, dc in next sc) twice; rep from * around, end last rep, sc in next dc, ch 3, join with a sl st to beg ch. (94 sts)

Rnds 8–9: Ch 4, *dc in next dc, ch 1, dc in next ch-3 sp, ch 1, dc in next sc, ch 1, dc in next ch-3 sp; rep from * around, join with a sl st to beg ch.

Rnd 10: As rnd 2.

Rnd 11: Ch 4, dc in same st as join, *ch 3, sk next 3 dc, sc in next dc, ch 3, sk next 3 dc, (dc, ch 1, dc) in next sc, (ch 3, sk next 3 dc, sc in next dc, ch 3, sk next 3 dc, dc in next sc) 4 times; rep from * around, end last rep, sc in next dc, ch 3, join with a sl st to beg ch. (110 sts)

Rnds 12–13: Ch 4, *dc in next dc, ch 1, dc in next ch-3 sp, ch 1, dc in next sc, ch 1, dc in next ch-3 sp; rep from * around, join with a sl st to beg ch.

Rnd 14: As rnd 2.

Rnd 15: Ch 4, dc in same st as join, *ch 3, sk next 3 dc, sc in next dc, ch 3, sk next 3 dc, (dc, ch 1, dc) in next sc, (ch 3, sk next 3 dc, sc in next dc, ch 3, sk next 3 dc, dc in next sc) 4 times; rep from * around, end last rep, sc in next dc, ch 3, join with a sl st to beg ch. (126 sts)

Rnds 16–17: Ch 4, *dc in next dc, ch 1, dc in next ch-3 sp, ch 1, dc in next sc, ch 1, dc in next ch-3 sp; rep from * around, join with a sl st to beg ch.

Rnd 18: As rnd 2. Fasten off.

Pin and block to measurements. Weave in ends.

Beginner

Intermediate

Advanced

SIDE-TO-SIDE SHAWLS

The side-to-side shawl is one of my favorite constructions. Increases and decreases are usually worked along one side of the shawl to create the shape desired, whether circular, triangular, or crescent. This is also a great way to work in simple patterns and play with yarn!

We begin with a simple one-skein side-to-side shawl worked in a loose gauge to let the yarn do all the work. Second, we'll play with yarn, the best way we know how, with our hook, combining yarns for a fun and easy shawl that combines stitch patterns. Then we move onto a glitzy number with multiple stitch patterns that make it interesting yet not overcomplicated.

BASIC SIDE-TO-SIDE SHAWL

Side-to-side shawls are great for showing off that one skein of beautiful yarn. This shawl uses simple increases and decreases to give it a classic crescent shape.

SKILL LEVEL
Beginner

FINISHED MEASUREMENTS
Wingspan: 120 in. (305 cm)
Depth: 12 in. (30 cm)

YARN
Lion Brand Yarn Scarfie (78% acrylic, 22% wool; 312 yd./285 m per 5.3 oz./150 g skein)
- 1 skein Cream/Silver

HOOK & OTHER MATERIALS
- US J-10 (6 mm) crochet hook
- Yarn needle
- Scissors

GAUGE
In half double crochet, 7 sts x 2.5 rows = 2 in. (5 cm) square
Adjust hook size if necessary to obtain gauge.

NOTES
- Ch 2 does not count as hdc throughout.

Instructions

Ch 3.

Row 1 (RS): Hdc in 3rd st from hook.

Row 2 (WS): Ch 2, turn, 3 hdc in hdc.

Row 3: Ch 2, turn, 2 hdc in first st, hdc in each st across.

Row 4: Ch 2, turn, hdc in each st across.

Rep rows 3 and 4 until shawl is 12 in. (30 cm) wide, or desired
  depth; end after working a WS row.

Next row: Ch 2, turn, hdc2tog in first 2 sts, hdc in each st across.

Next row: Ch 2, turn, hdc in each st across.

Rep last 2 rows until 1 st remains. Fasten off.

Pin and block to measurements. Weave in ends.

PURPLE MOSS SHAWL

One great way to give interest and dimension to shawls is by holding two strands of yarn together. By using a very lightweight fingering-weight yarn such as mohair, the gauge is not affected!

SKILL LEVEL
Intermediate

FINISHED MEASUREMENTS
Wingspan: 56 in. (142 cm)
Depth: 12 in. (30 cm)

YARN
Lion Brand Yarn Vanna's Choice, worsted-weight yarn (100% acrylic; 170 yd./156 m per 3.5 oz./100 g skein)
- 1 skein Eggplant

Lion Brand Yarn LB Collection Silk Mohair, fingering-weight yarn (70% Super Kid Mohair, 30% silk; 231 yd./212 m per 0.88 oz./25 g skein)
- 1 skein Iris

HOOK & OTHER MATERIALS
- US J-10 (6 mm) crochet hook
- Yarn needle
- Scissors

GAUGE
In double crochet, 6 sts x 3 rows = 2 in. (5 cm) square
Adjust hook size if necessary to obtain gauge.

NOTES
- Ch 3 counts as dc throughout.
- Ch 4 counts as (dc, ch 1) throughout.

With 1 strand of each yarn held together, ch 4.

Row 1 (RS): Dc in 4th ch from hook. (2 dc)

Row 2 (WS): Ch 3, turn, 3 dc in dc. (4 dc)

Row 3 (RS): Ch 3, turn, dc in first st, dc in each st across. (5 dc)

Row 4 (WS): Ch 3, turn, dc in each st across to last 2 sts, 2 dc in next st, dc in last dc. (6 dc)

Rep last 2 rows until shawl is 12 in. deep. (22 dc)

Drop the silk mohair lightweight yarn. End after working a WS Row.

Next row (RS): Ch 4, turn, *(dc, ch 1) in next st, sk next dc; rep from * across to last 2 dc, dc in last dc. (12 dc, 11 ch-1 sps)

Next row (WS): Ch 4, turn, *ch 1, dc; rep from * across to last dc, (ch 1, dc) in last dc. (23 dc)

Rep last 2 rows until shawl is 12 in. (30 cm) in depth. Drop 1 strand of yarn. End after working a WS row.

Next row (RS): Ch 3, turn, dc in first dc, dc2tog, dc in each dc across.

Next row (WS): Ch 3, turn, dc in each dc across to last 3 sts, dc2tog, dc in last dc.

Rep last 2 rows until 21 sts rem.

Next row (RS): Ch 4, turn, dc2tog, *dc in next dc, ch 1, sk next dc; rep from * across to last dc, dc in last dc.

Next row (WS): Ch 4, turn, *dc in next dc, ch 1; rep from * across to last dc, dc in last dc.

Rep last 2 rows until 1 st remains.

Pin and block to measurements. Weave in ends.

WANDERING SUNSET SHAWL

This gorgeous side-to-side shawl uses a very old form of shaping that will make it lie on your shoulders just right. Make this in a heavier-weight yarn for a dramatic and fashionable winter accessory.

SKILL LEVEL
Advanced

FINISHED MEASUREMENTS
Wingspan: 56 in. (142 cm)
Depth: 12 in. (30 cm)

YARN
Lion Brand Yarn Vanna's Glamour, sport-weight yarn (96% acrylic, 4% metallic polyester; 202 yd./185 m per 1.75 oz./50 g skein)
- 2 skeins Purple Topaz

HOOK & OTHER MATERIALS
- US J-10 (6 mm) crochet hook
- Yarn needle
- Scissors

GAUGE
In double crochet, 6 sts x 3.5 rows = 2 in. (5 cm) square
Adjust hook size if necessary to obtain gauge.

NOTES
- Ch 3 counts as dc throughout.
- Ch 4 counts as (dc, ch 1) throughout.

Instructions

Ch 17.

Row 1 (RS): Dc in 4th ch from hook, *ch 1, sk next st, dc in next st; rep from * across to last st, ch 1, 3 dc in last st. (11 dc, 8 ch-1 sps)

Row 2 (WS): Ch 3, turn, 2 dc in next st, dc next st, *ch 1, sk next st, dc in next dc; rep from * across. (11 dc, 8 ch-1 sps)

Row 3 (RS): Ch 4, turn, dc in next dc, (ch 1, dc in next dc) 7 times, 2 dc in next dc, dc in each st across. (12 dc, 8 ch-1 sps)

Row 4: Ch 3, turn, dc in each dc across to 2 sts before first ch-1 sp, 2 dc in next dc, (dc in next dc, ch 1) 8 times, dc in last dc. (13 dc, 8 ch-1 sps)

Rep rows 3 and 4 a further 17 times.

Next 5 rows: Ch 4, turn, dc in next dc, *ch 1, dc in next dc; rep from * across.

Next row: Ch 4, turn, dc in next dc, (ch 1, dc in next dc) 7 times, dc in next dc, dc2tog, dc in each st across.

Next row: Ch 3, turn, dc in each dc across to 3 sts before first ch-1 sp, dc2tog, (dc in next dc, ch 1) 8 times, dc in last dc.

Rep last 2 rows until 1 st rem.

Pin and block to measurements. Weave in ends.

Beginner

Intermediate

Advanced

SQUARE SHAWLS

Square shawls can be worked in a number of ways and feature a number of different techniques. From the traditional granny square to more lacy numbers, these shawls are a great example of how to take a rather simple shape and make it work for all crocheters.

In this chapter we'll go back to basics with a simple granny-square shawl, with a twist. Then we'll move on to a worsted-weight shawl with a drop of sun. Lastly we'll dive headfirst into lace!

BASIC SQUARE SHAWL

Square shawls are just awesome. If you can make a basic granny square, you can make this shawl. Work it with a bunch of different yarns as I did, or choose your own for a fun and innovative shawl.

SKILL LEVEL
Beginner

FINISHED MEASUREMENTS
Wingspan: 48 in. (122 cm)
Depth: 15 in. (38 cm)

YARN
Lion Brand Yarn Vanna's Choice, worsted-weight yarn (80% acrylic, 20% wool; 106 yd./97 m per 6 oz./170 g skein)
- 1 skein A (Light Blue)
- 1 skein B (Sky Blue)
- 1 skein C (Midnight Blue)

HOOK & OTHER MATERIALS
- US L-11 (8 mm) crochet hook
- Yarn needle
- Scissors

GAUGE
Two 3-dc groups x 2 rows = 2 in. (5 cm) square
Adjust hook size if necessary to obtain gauge.

NOTES
- Ch 4 counts as (dc, ch 1) throughout.

Instructions

Starting with A, Ch 4.

Row 1: (3 dc, ch 2, 3 dc, ch 2, 3 dc, ch 1, dc) in 4th ch from hook.

Row 2: Ch 4, turn, 3 dc in first ch-1 sp, ch 1, (3 dc, ch 3, 3 dc, ch 1) in next 2 ch-2 sps, 3 dc in last ch-1 sp, ch 1, dc in last st.

Row 3: Ch 4, turn, 3 dc in first ch-1 sp, *ch 1, 3 dc in next ch-1 sp, ch 1, (3 dc, ch 3, 3 dc) in next ch-3 sp; rep from * once more, ch 1, 3 dc in next ch-1 sp, ch 1, 3 dc in last ch-1 sp, dc in last st.

Row 4: Ch 4, turn, *3 dc in each ch-1 sp to first ch-3 sp, (3 dc, ch 3, 3 dc) in next ch-3 sp; rep from * once more; then work 3 dc in each ch-1 sp to end, dc in last st.

Work with Color A for 15 rows. Change to B for 6 rows. Change to C for 2 rows.

If desired, end shawl by working dc in each st and ch-sp around.

Rep row 4 until shawl is 48 in. (122 cm) or desired wingspan.

Pin and block to measurements. Weave in ends.

SUNSHINE SQUARED SHAWL

This shawl builds on our square method of shaping and incorporates three different stitch patterns. Each of the stitch patterns builds on its predecessor, making this a fun and interesting shawl to stitch.

SKILL LEVEL
Intermediate

FINISHED MEASUREMENTS
Wingspan: 40 in. (102 cm)
Depth: 14 in. (36 cm)

YARN
Lion Brand Yarn Vanna's Choice, worsted-weight yarn (100% acrylic; 170 yd./156 m per 3.5 oz./100 g skein)
- 2 skeins Duckie

HOOK & OTHER MATERIALS
- US L-11 (8 mm) crochet hook
- Yarn needle
- Scissors

GAUGE
In pattern stitch, two 3-dc groups x 2 rows = 2 in. (5 cm) square
Adjust hook size if necessary to obtain gauge.

NOTES
- Ch 4 counts as (dc, ch 1) throughout.

Instructions

Ch 4.

Row 1: (3 dc, ch 2, 3 dc, ch 2, 3 dc, ch 1, dc) in 4th ch from hook.

Row 2: Ch 4, turn, 3 dc in first ch-1 sp, ch 1, (3 dc, ch 3, 3 dc, ch 1) in next 2 ch-2 sps, 3 dc in last ch-1 sp, ch 1, dc in last st.

Row 3: Ch 4, turn, 3 dc in first ch-1 sp, *ch 1, 3 dc in next ch-1 sp, ch 1, (3 dc, ch 3, 3 dc) in next ch-3 sp; rep from * once more, ch 1, 3 dc in next ch-1 sp, ch 1, 3 dc in last ch-1 sp, dc in last st.

Row 4: Ch 4, turn, *3 dc in each ch-1 sp to first ch-3 sp, (3 dc, ch 3, 3 dc) in next ch-3 sp; rep from * once more, then work 3 dc in each ch-1 sp to end, dc in last st.

Row 5: Ch 4, turn, *(1 dc, ch 1, 1 dc) in each ch-1 sp to first ch-3 sp, (3 dc, ch 3, 3 dc) in next ch-3 sp; rep from * once more, then work (1 dc, ch 1, 1 dc) in each ch-1 sp to end, dc in last st.

Rep row 5, 3 more times.

Row 9: Ch 4, turn, *(1 dc, ch 2) in each ch-1 sp to first ch-3 sp, (3 dc, ch 3, 3 dc) in next ch-3 sp; rep from * once more, then work (1 dc, ch 2) in each ch-1 sp to end, dc in last st.

Rep row 9, 3 more times.

Rep row 4 until shawl is 40 in. (102 cm) or desired wingspan.

Pin and block to measurements. Weave in ends.

CURRANT SHAWL

A stunning openwork lace shawl is made approachable with a worsted-weight yarn. Using an 8 mm hook gives us the drape and lightness we look for in a shawl like this.

SKILL LEVEL
Advanced

FINISHED MEASUREMENTS
Wingspan: 40 in. (102 cm)
Depth: 17 in. (43 cm)

YARN
Lion Brand Yarn Heartland, worsted-weight yarn (100% acrylic; 251 yd./230 m per 5 oz./142 g skein)
- 1 skein Redwood

HOOK & OTHER MATERIALS
- US L-11 (8 mm) crochet hook
- Yarn needle
- Scissors

GAUGE
In treble crochet, 3 tr x 2 rows = 2 in. (5 cm) square
Adjust hook size if necessary to obtain gauge.

NOTES
- Ch 4 counts as tr throughout.

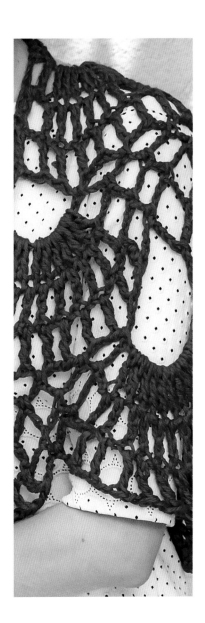

Instructions

Ch 4, join in a small circle.

Row 1: Ch 4, 17 tr in center of ring.

Row 2: Ch 4, turn, tr in next st, *ch 10, sk next 4 sts, tr in each of the next 2 tr; rep from * to end.

Row 3: Ch 4, turn, tr in next st, *ch 2, (tr in next st, ch 1) 10 times into ch-10 sp, ch 1, tr in each of the next 2 tr; rep from * across.

Row 4: Ch 4, turn, tr in next st, *ch 2, (tr in next st, ch 2) 10 times, ch 1, tr in each of the next 2 tr; rep from * across.

Row 5: Ch 4, turn, tr in next st, *ch 10, sk two ch-2 sps, (sc in next ch-2 sp, ch 5, sk next ch-2 sp) 3 times, sc in next ch-2 sp, ch 10, tr in each of the next 2 tr; rep from * across.

Row 6: Ch 4, turn, tr in next st, *10 tr in next ch-10 sp, (ch 5, sc in next ch-5 sp) 3 times, ch 5, 10 tr in next ch-10 sp, ch 1, tr in each of the next 2 tr; rep from * across.

Row 7: Ch 4, turn, tr in next st, *ch 1, (tr in next st, ch 1) 10 times, ch 5, (sc in next ch-5 sp, ch 5) twice, ch 5, (tr in next st, ch 1) 10 times, ch 1, tr in each of the next 2 tr; rep from * across.

Row 8: Ch 4, turn, tr in next st, *ch 2, (tr in next st, ch 2) 10 times, ch 5, sc in next ch-5 sp, ch 5, (tr in next st, ch 2) 10 times, ch 1, tr in each of the next 2 tr; rep from * across.

Rep rows 5–8 until shawl is 40 in. (102 cm) or desired wingspan. Fasten off.

Pin and block to measurements. Weave in ends.

Beginner

Intermediate

Advanced

WEDGE SHAWLS

The wedge shawl, also sometimes referred to as a crescent shawl, is similar in shape to the pi shawl but different in construction. Distinct points of increase are used on each shawl to create the overall shape. Think of it like working a few top-down triangle shawls at the same time. It's the same style, just a little different. Did I mention they are fun? Lots of fun!

A quick-to-stitch lacy shawl is what we'll start with, working in a fingering-weight yarn; this piece can be upsized by using a worsted-weight or bulky-weight yarn. Worsted-weight held double makes our next shawl a quick and cozy make. The advanced shawl is nice and big but using a large hook keeps it airy and light even though knit in a bulky yarn.

BASIC WEDGE SHAWL

A wedge shawl, while similar to a pi shawl, is different in that it contains distinct increase points. This shawl is worked in fingering-weight yarn and a large hook for a quick-to-stitch yet lightweight accessory.

SKILL LEVEL
Beginner

FINISHED MEASUREMENTS
Wingspan: 48 in. (122 cm)
Depth: 14 in. (36 cm)

YARN
Lion Brand Yarn Sock-Ease, fingering-weight
  yarn (75% wool, 25% nylon; 438 yd./400 m per
  3.5 oz./100 g skein)
  ■ 1 skein A (Marshmallow)
  ■ 1 skein B (Snow Cone)

HOOK & OTHER MATERIALS
  ■ US H-8 (5 mm) crochet hook
  ■ Yarn needle
  ■ Scissors

GAUGE
In half double crochet, 6 sts x 5 rows = 2 in.
  (5 cm) square
Adjust hook size if necessary to obtain gauge.

NOTES
  ■ Ch 2 does not count as hdc throughout.

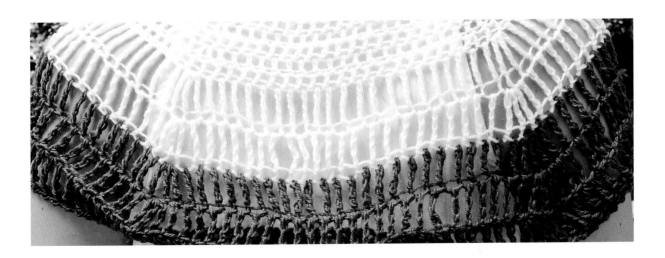

Instructions

With A, ch 3.

Row 1: 8 hdc in 3rd ch from hook. (8 hdc)

Row 2: Ch 2, turn, 2 hdc in each st across. (16 hdc)

Row 3: Ch 2, turn, *2 hdc in next st, hdc in next st; rep from * across to last st, 2 hdc in last hdc. (24 hdc)

Row 4: Ch 2, turn, *2 hdc in next st, hdc in each of the next 2 sts; rep from * across to last st, 2 hdc in last hdc. (32 hdc)

Row 5: Ch 2, turn, *2 hdc in next st, hdc in each of the next 3 sts; rep from * across to last st, 2 hdc in last hdc. (40 hdc)

Rep Row 5 an additional 16 times for a total of 21 rows.

Change to B, if desired.

Next row: Ch 5, dtr in each st across, working 3 dtr in between each of the increase sts. (10 sts inc)

Repeat last row, 2 more times. Fasten off.

Pin and block to measurements. Weave in ends.

ROSE BLOSSOM SHAWL

This chunky wedge shawl is a definite statement piece. Worsted-weight yarn held double makes for a quick project.

SKILL LEVEL
Intermediate

FINISHED MEASUREMENTS
Wingspan: 40 in. (102 cm)
Depth: 16 in. (41 cm)

YARN
Lion Brand Yarn Wool-Ease, worsted-weight yarn (75% wool, 25% nylon; 197 yd./180 m per 3 oz./85 g skein)
- 4 skeins Ranch Red

HOOK & OTHER MATERIALS
- US N/P-15 (10 mm) crochet hook
- Yarn needle
- Scissors

GAUGE
In pattern stitch, 4 sts x 1 row = 2 in. (5 cm) square
Adjust hook size if necessary to obtain gauge.

NOTES
- Ch 4 counts as tr throughout.

Instructions

With 2 strands held together, ch 5.

Row 1: 2 tr in 5th ch from hook, (ch 1, 3 tr) 3 times into same ch. (four 3-tr groups)

Row 2: Ch 4, turn, 2 tr in same st, (ch 1, 3 tr, ch 3, 3 tr) in each ch-1 sp across, ch 1, 3 tr in last st.

Row 3: Ch 4, turn, 2 tr in same st, *ch 1, tr in next ch-1 sp, (ch 1, 3 tr, ch 1, 3 tr) in next ch-3 sp; rep from * twice more, ch 1, tr in next ch-1 sp, 3 tr in last st.

Row 4: Ch 4, turn, 2 tr in same st, *ch 1, tr in each ch-1 sp to next ch-3 sp, (ch 1, 3 tr, ch 1, 3 tr) in next ch-3 sp; rep from * across, ch 1, tr in each ch-1 sp to end, 3 tr in last st.

Rep row 4, 7 more times. Fasten off.

Pin and block to measurements. Weave in ends.

ARUM SHAWL

A bulky-weight yarn and a larger hook give this shawl a lightweight look and feel without being too feather light.

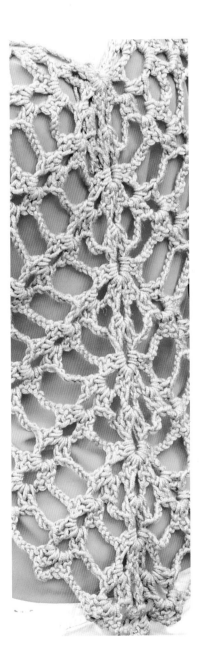

SKILL LEVEL
Advanced

FINISHED MEASUREMENTS
Wingspan: 40 in. (102 cm)
Depth: 24 in. (61 cm)

YARN
Lion Brand Yarn Lion's Pride Woolspun, bulky-weight yarn (80% acrylic, 20% wool; 124 yd./116 m per 3.5 oz./100 g skein)
- 2 skeins Honey

HOOK & OTHER MATERIALS
- US L-11 (8 mm) crochet hook
- Yarn needle
- Scissors

GAUGE
In double crochet, 2 sts x 2 rows = 2 in. (5 cm) square
Adjust hook size if necessary to obtain gauge.

NOTES
- Ch 6 counts as (dc, ch 2) throughout.

Ch 5.

Row 1: Tr in 5th ch from hook, (ch 2, 2 tr) 5 times into same ch.

Row 2: Ch 6, turn, 2 tr in first ch-2 sp, *ch 2, (2 tr, ch 2, 2 tr) in next ch-2 sp; rep from * across to last ch-2 sp, 2 tr in last ch-2 sp, ch 2, tr in last st.

Row 3: Ch 6, turn, 2 tr in first ch-2 sp, (ch 2, [2 tr, ch 2, 2 tr] in next ch-2 sp) twice, ([2 tr, ch 2] 3 times, 2 tr) in next ch-2 sp, (ch 2, [2 tr, ch 2, 2 tr] in next ch-2 sp) twice, ch 2, 2 tr in last st.

Row 4 and all even rows: Ch 6, turn, *(2 tr, ch 2, 2 tr) in next ch-2 sp, ch 5; rep from * across to last ch-2 sp, (2 tr, ch 2, 2 tr) in last ch-2 sp.

Row 5: Ch 6, turn, 2 tr in first ch-2 sp, (ch 2, [2 tr, ch 2, 2 tr] in next ch-2 sp) 4 times more, ([2 tr, ch 2] 3 times, 2 tr) in next ch-2 sp, (ch 2, [2 tr, ch 2, 2 tr] in next ch-2 sp) 4 times more, ch 2, 2 tr in last st.

Row 7: Ch 6, turn, 2 tr in first ch-2 sp, (ch 2, [2 tr, ch 2, 2 tr] in next ch-2 sp) 6 times more, ([2 tr, ch 2] 3 times, 2 tr) in next ch-2 sp, (ch 2, [2 tr, ch 2, 2 tr] in next ch-2 sp), 6 times more, ch 2, 2 tr in last st.

Row 9: Ch 6, turn, 2 tr in first ch-2 sp, (ch 2, [2 tr, ch 2, 2 tr] in next ch-2 sp) 8 times more, ([2 tr, ch 2] 3 times, 2 tr) in next ch-2 sp, (ch 2, [2 tr, ch 2, 2 tr] in next ch-2 sp), 8 times more, ch 2, 2 tr in last st.

Row 11: Ch 6, turn, 2 tr in first ch-2 sp, (ch 2, [2 tr, ch 2, 2 tr] in next ch-2 sp) 10 times more, ([2 tr, ch 2] 3 times, 2 tr) in next ch-2 sp, (ch 2, [2 tr, ch 2, 2 tr] in next ch-2 sp), 10 times more, ch 2, 2 tr in last st.

Row 13: Ch 6, turn, 2 tr in first ch-2 sp, (ch 2, [2 tr, ch 2, 2 tr] in next ch-2 sp) 12 times more, ([2 tr, ch 2] 3 times, 2 tr) in next ch-2 sp, (ch 2, [2 tr, ch 2, 2 tr] in next ch-2 sp), 12 times more, ch 2, 2 tr in last st.

Row 15: Ch 6, turn, 2 tr in first ch-2 sp, (ch 2, [2 tr, ch 2, 2 tr] in next ch-2 sp) 14 times more, ([2 tr, ch 2] 3 times, 2 tr) in next ch-2 sp, (ch 2, [2 tr, ch 2, 2 tr] in next ch-2 sp), 14 times more, ch 2, 2 tr in last st. Fasten off.

Pin and block to measurements. Weave in ends.

Beginner

Intermediate

Advanced

TOP-DOWN TRIANGLE SHAWLS

Different from the bottom-up triangle shawl, top-down triangle shawls are worked with increases in the center and at each end. This gives you the ability to create a patterned, and quite gorgeous, crochet shawl that is as interesting to make as it is to wear. They also stitch up quite fast.

A granny triangle starts us off with a burst of color. Next we use a bulky yarn and large hook to make a super-fast shawl that you'll make again and again. Lastly, we'll work on a lacy shawl with a fun-to-stitch motif!

BASIC TOP-DOWN TRIANGLE SHAWL

If bottom-up triangle shawls aren't your cup of tea, try top down! This shawl begins at the neck and works out with increases in each row. It makes for a fun and fast piece.

SKILL LEVEL
Beginner

FINISHED MEASUREMENTS
Wingspan: 48 in. (122 cm)
Depth: 24 in. (61 cm)

YARN
Lion Brand Yarn Vanna's Choice, worsted-weight yarn (100% acrylic;
  170 yd./156 m per 3.5 oz./100 g skein)
- 2 skeins A (Fisherman)
- 2 skeins B (Fern)
- 2 skeins C (Raspberry)

HOOK & OTHER MATERIALS
- US J-10 (6 mm) crochet hook
- Yarn needle
- Scissors

GAUGE
In double crochet, 3 sts x 1 row = 1 in. (2.5 cm) square
Adjust hook size if necessary to obtain gauge.

NOTES
- Ch 4 counts as (dc, ch 1) throughout.

Instructions

With A, ch 4.

Row 1: 3 dc in 4th ch from hook, ch 3, 3 dc in same ch, ch 1, dc in same ch.

Row 2: Ch 4, turn, 3 dc in first ch-1 sp, ch 1, (3 dc, ch 3, 3 dc) in next ch-3 sp, ch 1, 3 dc in last ch-1 sp, ch 1, dc in top of t-ch.

Row 3: Ch 4, turn, 3 dc in first ch-1 sp, ch 1, 3 dc in next ch-1 sp, ch 1, (3 dc, ch 3, 3 dc) in next ch-3 sp, ch 1, 3 dc in next ch-1 sp, ch 1, 3 dc in last ch-1 sp, ch 1, dc in top of t-ch.

Continue as established, working one 3-dc group into each ch-1 sp across and one (3 dc, ch 3, 3 dc) group into ch-3 sp, until shawl is desired width. Fasten off.

If you wish to change colors as shown in photo, work as follows:
Rows 1–11: Color A
Rows 12–13: Color B
Rows 14–15: Color C
Rows 16–17: Color B
Rows 18–19: Color C
Rows 20–21: Color B
Row 22: Color C

Pin and block to measurements. Weave in ends.

HYDRANGEA SHAWL

This top-down triangle shawl is one of my favorites. The shawl is worked from the neck down with a fun-to-stitch lace section. A simple edge completes the shawl perfectly.

SKILL LEVEL
Intermediate

FINISHED MEASUREMENTS
Wingspan: 48 in. (122 cm)
Depth: 24 in. (61 cm)

YARN
Lion Brand Yarn Sock-Ease, fingering-weight yarn (75% wool, 25% nylon; 438 yd./400 m per 3.5 oz./100 g skein)
- 1 skein Lollipop

HOOK & OTHER MATERIALS
- US H-8 (5 mm) crochet hook
- Yarn needle
- Scissors

GAUGE
In pattern stitch (filet double crochet: dc, ch 1, dc), 14 sts x 12 rows = 4 in. (10 cm) square
Adjust hook size if necessary to obtain gauge.

NOTES
- Shawl can be made larger or smaller depending on the amount of rows worked in the filet crochet section. If a larger shawl is desired, simply work more rows to desired wingspan.

SPECIAL STITCHES

Half shell: 3 dc into same st.
Open half shell: (1 dc, ch 1, 1 dc) into same st.
Shell: 5 dc in same st.
Top of shell: This refers to the central stitch of the shell, or the 3rd st. You will only ever work into the top of a shell and can discount all other stitches in the shell when working.

Instructions

SECTION 1

Ch 6.

Row 1: 3 dc in 4th ch from hook, (ch 2, 3 dc in next ch) twice. (9 dc)

Row 2: Ch 3, half shell in first st, ch 2, sk 2 dc, 3 dc in ch-2 sp, ch 2, sk 1 dc, shell, ch 2, sk 1 dc, 3 dc in ch-2 sp, ch 2, sk 2 dc, half shell in last st. (17 dc)

Row 3: Ch 3, half shell in first st, *ch 2, 2 dc in ch-2 sp, dc in each dc to next ch-2 sp, 2 dc in ch-2 sp, ch 2** shell in top of shell; rep from * to **, half shell in last st.

Repeat row 3 a total of 10 times. You will now have 43 dc in between the ch-2 sps on each side.

SECTION 2

Row 1: Ch 3, half shell in first st, ch 2, sk ch-2 sp, *half shell, ch 1, sk 1 dc; rep from * to last st before ch-2 sp, half shell in last st, ch 2**, shell in top of shell, ch 2, sk ch-2 sp, half shell, ch 1, sk 1 dc; rep from * to **, half shell in last st.

Repeat row 1 until shawl is the desired width when measured from side to side. Recommended width is 48 in. (122 cm). Do keep in mind that blocking will add some length.

SECTION 3

Row 1: Ch 3, half shell in first st, ch 2, sk ch-2 sp, *shell in next ch-1 sp, sk 2 ch-1 sps, ch 3, rep from * to last st before ch-2 sp, last shell in last st, ch 2**, shell in top of shell, ch 2, sk ch-2 sp, rep from * to **, half shell in last st.

Row 2: Ch 3, half shell in first st, ch 2, sk ch-2 sp, *dc in each dc of shell, sk 2 ch-1 sps, ch 3, rep from * to last st before ch-2 sp, last shell in last st, ch 2**, shell in top of shell, ch 2, sk ch-2 sp, rep from * to **, half shell in last st.

Repeat rows 1 and 2, and then row 1. Fasten off.

Pin and block to measurements. Weave in ends.

CYCLAMEN SHAWL

This gorgeous lace shawl is worked from the top down in a challenging lace pattern. The hardest part is at the beginning. Once you get to the repeat, it's as easy as pie!

SKILL LEVEL
Advanced

FINISHED MEASUREMENTS
Wingspan: 48 in. (122 cm)
Depth: 24 in. (61 cm)

YARN
Lion Brand Yarn Sock-Ease, fingering-weight yarn (75% wool, 25% nylon; 438 yd./400 m per 3.5 oz./100 g skein)
- 1 skein Marshmallow

HOOK & OTHER MATERIALS
- US H-8 (5 mm) crochet hook
- Yarn needle
- Scissors

GAUGE
In pattern stitch, 14 sts x 12 rows = 4 in. (10 cm) square
Adjust hook size if necessary to obtain gauge.

NOTES
- Shawl can be made larger or smaller depending on the amount of rows worked. If a larger shawl is desired, simply work more rows to desired wingspan.
- Ch 5 counts at (tr, ch 1) throughout.

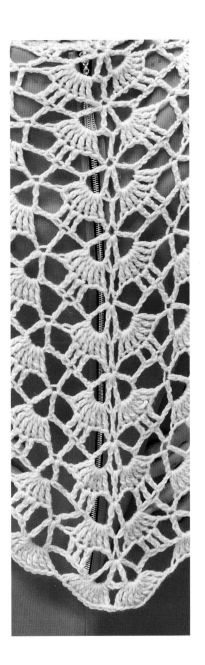

Instructions

Ch 4.

Row 1: Tr in 4th ch from hook, (ch 3, 2 tr, ch 3, 2 tr) in same ch.

Row 2: Ch 5, turn, 7 tr in next ch-3 sp, ch 1, tr in between next 2 tr, ch 1, 7 tr in next ch-3 sp, ch 1, tr in last st.

Row 3: Ch 5, turn, (tr, ch 3, tr) in first st, ch 1, sk next 2 tr, tr in each of the next 3 tr, ch 1, sk next 2 tr, (tr, ch 3, tr, ch 1, tr, ch 3, tr) in next tr, ch 1, sk next 2 tr, tr in each of the next 3 tr, ch 1, sk next 2 tr, (tr, ch 3, tr, ch 1, tr) in last st.

Row 4: Ch 5, turn, 7 tr in next ch-3 sp, ch 1, sk next tr, tr in next tr, ch 1, 7 tr in next ch-3 sp, ch 1, tr in next ch-1 sp, ch 1, 7 tr in next ch-3 sp, ch 1, sk next tr, tr in next tr, ch 1, 7 tr in next ch-3 sp, ch 1, tr in last st.

Row 5: Ch 5, turn, *(tr, ch 3, tr) in next ch-1 sp, ch 1, sk 1 tr, tr in each of the next 3 tr, ch 1; rep from * twice more, (tr, ch 3, tr, ch 1, tr, ch 3, tr) in next tr, ch 1, *(tr, ch 3, tr) in next ch-1 sp, ch 1, sk 1 tr, tr in each of the next 3 tr, ch 1; rep from * twice more, ch 1, (tr, ch 3, tr, ch 1, tr) in last st.

Row 6: Ch 5, turn, *7 tr in next ch-3 sp, ch 1, sk next tr, tr in next tr; rep from * twice more, ch 1, tr in ch-1 sp, ch 1, 7 tr in next ch-3 sp, ch 1, sk next tr, tr in next tr; rep from * twice more, ch 1, tr in last st.

Row 7: Ch 5, turn, *(tr, ch 3, tr) in next ch-1 sp, ch 1, sk 1 tr, tr in each of the next 3 tr, ch 1; rep from * 3 times more, (tr, ch 3, tr, ch 1, tr, ch 3, tr) in next tr, ch 1, *(tr, ch 3, tr) in next ch-1 sp, ch 1, sk 1 tr, tr in each of the next 3 tr, ch 1; rep from * 3 times more, ch 1, (tr, ch 3, tr, ch 1, tr) in last st.

Continue in this manner, repeating rows 6 and 7 until shawl measures 48 in. (122 cm) in length or desired wingspan.

Pin and block to measurements. Weave in ends.

ABBREVIATIONS / STITCH GUIDE

beg	beginning
ch	chain: Make a slipknot on hook. Yarn over hook from back to front and grab it with hook; draw hooked yarn through slipknot and onto hook. One chain made.
ch-sp	chain space(s)
cm	centimeter(s)
dc	double crochet: Yarn over hook from back to front. Insert hook into indicated stitch of previous row. Yarn over hook; pull yarn through the stitch—3 loops on hook. Yarn over hook; pull yarn through first 2 loops on the hook—2 loops remain on hook. Yarn over hook, pull yarn through 2 loops on hook. One loop remains on hook; one double crochet made.
dc2tog	double crochet 2 together: To make this dec stitch, yarn over hook from back to front. Insert hook into indicated stitch. Yarn over hook; pull yarn through the stitch—3 loops on hook. Yarn over hook; pull yarn through first 2 loops on the hook—2 loops remain on hook. Yarn over hook—3 loops on hook. Insert hook into next stitch. Yarn over, pull yarn through stitch—4 sts on hook; yarn over, pull through first 2 loops on hook. Yarn over, pull through all 3 loops on hook. One loop remains on hook; one double crochet 2 together made.

dtr	double treble: Yarn over hook 3 times; insert hook into stitch as directed, yarn over and draw through stitch. Yarn over and draw through 2 loops on the hook 4 times.
g	gram(s)
hdc	half double crochet: Yarn over hook. Insert hook into designated chain; yarn over, draw yarn through stitch—3 loops on hook. Yarn over; pull through all 3 loops on hook. One loop on hook; one half double crochet complete.
hdc2tog	half double crochet 2 together: To make this dec stitch, insert hook into designated stitch in previous row, yarn over, pull yarn through stitch—2 sts on hook. Insert hook into next stitch, yarn over and draw through stitch—3 sts on hook. Yarn over and pull yarn through all 3 loops on hook. One half double crochet 2 together complete; 2 sts are now 1.
in.	inch(es)
inc	increase(d)
m	meter(s)
mm	millimeter(s)
oz.	ounce(s)
rep	repeat

rnd(s)	round(s)
RS	right side
sc	single crochet: Insert hook into indicated stitch, yarn over hook from back to front and pull through stitch so there are two loops on the hook, and yarn over hook from back to front and pull through both loops on hook. One single crochet made.
sk	skip
sl st	slip stitch(es)
sp/sps	space(s)
st/sts	stitch(es)
t-ch	turning chain
tr	treble crochet: Yarn over hook 2 times; insert hook into stitch as directed, yarn over and draw through stitch—4 sts on hook. Yarn over and draw through 2 loops on the hook 3 times. One loop remains on hook; one treble crochet made.
Tdc	Tunisian double crochet: (forward pass, right to left) From the foundation row, ch 2. Yarn over and insert hook behind the next vertical bar. Yarn over and pull up a loop. Yarn over and pull through two loops on hook. Forward Tdc is complete; continue to work across the row. (return pass, left to right) *Do not turn the work.* Yarn over, pull through first loop on hook. Yarn over, draw through 2 loops; repeat.
Tss	Tunisian simple stitch: (forward pass, right to left) Insert hook into 2nd chain of foundation row from hook, yarn over, draw behind vertical bar to pull up a loop. Leave loop on hook. Repeat. (return pass, left to right) *Do not turn the work.* Yarn over, pull through first loop on hook. Yarn over, draw through 2 loops; repeat. (forward pass) Insert hook behind 2nd vertical bar of previous forward pass, yarn over, pull up a loop, insert hook behind next vertical bar, yarn over, pull up a loop. One Tunisian simple stitch made; repeat across the row.
WS	wrong side
yd.	yard(s)

VISUAL INDEX

Basic Poncho 61

Shifting Waves Poncho 65

Amaryllis Poncho 69

Basic Side-to-Side Shawl 75

Purple Moss Shawl 79

Wandering Sunset Shaw 83

Basic Square Shawl 89

Sunshine Squared Shawl 93

Currant Shawl 97

Basic Wedge Shawl 103

Rose Blossom Shawl 107

Arum Shawl 111

Basic Top-Down Triangle Shawl 117

Hydrangea Shawl 121

Cyclamen Shawl 125